Stumbled journey

Teresa Cabal

BookLeaf
Publishing

India | USA | UK

Presentation by *BookLeaf Publishing*

Web: www.bookleafpub.com

E-mail: info@bookleafpub.com

ISBN : 9789357448802

First edition 2021

Sundays

The emptiness of a Sunday
without silly dancing
goes away under the rain
over the checks coming.

Dethroned is the Monday
traditionally cursed
by normal people
keeping lips pursed.

For the heartbroken
the world heaviness
is better hidden
behind the daily stress.

What is it?

It is in the water
like it is in the air
like it is in your blood
feeding the burner.

You never had imaged
the amazing fire
you could create
just with your breath.

We are not dust
we are water
full of oxygen
we are water
full of fuel.

Shout and try harder
dance and relax
make it brighter
by breathing nicely.

Gone

Yesterday, I saw your face
In the middle of the crowd.
Without any empty space
I felt cowed.

I tried to call you
but my voice got lost
like I was a ghost
into the dark blue.

I tried to run
in order to reach you
but the fake wall I saw
made me feel paralysed.

It was only in my mind
with my deepest fears
I should let them behind
but I only get tears.

When I opened my eyes
I no longer saw you
neither the crowd
nor the wall.

My saddest truth
comes true:
You have gone
like a yawn.

Far away but here

Under my feet
there is nothing
but concrete.

Above my head,
full of dreams,
the stars spread.

Will we be alone?
Far away from
what is known.

We hardly can know
but I think
it´s not.

As you can see
the same stars
reflecting in the sea,
where I would like to be
dancing with you.

Hollow

Walking on the cliff
of the deepest sorrow
I found my feelings
extremely hollow.

It took me lots of time
to understand my truth,
knowing in tears
that I´ve lost my youth.

What you don´t know
it's all the sooth.
Maybe you imagine
but I know you don´t.

'Cause the indifference
you've shown
let my diffidence grow
but now it is mown.

Maybe never I though
this could be the end.
So sudden, so low
of you, as my friend.

Over twenty-five

Over twenty-five the horizon is further
from the wandered ways.
Oh! But this is murder!
and no one stays.

Everyone seeks a herder
who guide us through the maze
of the happiness.

Feel you

I am dying to feel
your lips on my skin,
knowing this is real.
This is no longer a dream.

Night falls in a cloudy sky
and I cannot see any star.
Soon the clouds´ll start to cry,
but they won´t wet my heart.

I am dying to touch
your skin under my hands.
Let me play in your back.
Here, or in other lands.

Walking my fate

The music of the creek
tinkles through the stones
that seems to speak.

Buried into the ground,
all my fears are dead
where they can´t be found.

Shadows creep
between the trees.
It´s no time to sleep.

I realize I´m not alone.
Nature is with me.
My strength has grown.

I belong to Earth,
looking for my fate
of only see ahead.

Walking through the path
of hundred thousand ways,
Should I use the map?

I´m reborn again,
released from the chains.
I don´t wanna feel more pain.

Magic

Playing with the wind
the revel fairies
wait for a hint
to jump into the cherries.

Magic is everywhere,
in every step you take
walking into the forest,
in everything you make
by following your heart.

Come

Come, come soon,
come and hide
within my blankets
come to my side.

Your clothes on the floor,
your skin attached to mine.
Please, take me there
where the world vanishes.

The lunges on a wooden table
wild and rushed,
provoking curves,
even glowing red,
miss the energy
of your quiet softness,
of your heartbeat
gushing through your eyes.

The spark

From the feet to the top of the head
without rush
warming all my tissues
like an oil lamp.

From the coast side,
a warm breeze
blows the surface of the skin
and stays to cheer.

From the guts to the breast,
the earthquake's center moves
shaking the nerves
and tickling the bones.

And from my toes to my thumbs,
baptised in that sea
more spicy than salty
waving away my breath.

Renaissance

It's in my dreams
where light awakes
like a radiance of the one
who once was staked.

Now, the fears are gone
from an innocent soul,
leaving the dark,
scaping the hole.

The latest renaissance,
believing, likely wrong,
but always strong,
that the truth has been found.

Finding the way

Ancient buildings
surround the view
lighted by the stars
which slowly grew.

Lost far away
from what was called home.
Finding the way
away from the roam.

Behind the black car

Shut up, shut up everyone!
Stop the music, silence the city!
Freeze the cars, and the trams!
Just stop, stop the city!

Stop the city and stop the world,
hold the breath and pause the life.
Everything is too loud.
I only need some time.

Some more time,
some more space,
more, more, more,
more to soothe my pace.

I can't hear myself,
the world is so noisy,
your silence is raucous,
your silence is brassy,
it's all I can listen.
Oh! For once let me cry!

I wanna loudly shout
and stop the world.

We follow you,
quiet than ever
we follow you,
we only wander
we'll follow you
hopefully later
we'll follow you
much later.

Humanilly

I don't have more time
to waste in sadness
bearing this world
plagued of madness.

Insanity of life
away from humanity
seems to be normal
in this raw reality.

Complicated existence
of serial machines
claiming more time
to be redeemed.

Last dance

Another day starts
feeling nothing
for broken hearts.

Hope departs
bored of waiting
for another chance.

Both parts
just thinking
of the last dance.

With you

What are you doing here,
where a long time ago
I used to be?

Just watching the show.
Will you come?

Of course,
but as long as
it's with you.

Goodbye

I said goodbye for you
I resigned the sweet amenity
of your loud caring,
of your warm company.

I loved you to the heart
couldn't find the melody.
I saw the stars in your eyes
but mine wasn't sparkly.

And I quietly left against my will
wishing for you to stay
just manuring your life
so I can be in your reality.

All my wishes come true,
you got who to smile at
and I vanished,
your rage disappeared
so did I,
songs brought your name
and kicked away mine.

You deserved that
I wanted to toast,

but you broke my glass
and I got bleeding cuts.

You stabbed my chest
since then I am lost
I found no land to fight for
my queen abdicated
and my God became atheist.

I said goodbye because of love
and it turned against me
disarmed love without passion
passion swings the saber
and beheads me.

Colors

Dark black, brown and blue
covering the canvas
doesn't matter the figures
but the intensity, full saturation.

A swing of the brush
Switch the tone
Bright red and yellow sprinkles
Keep intensity, full saturation.

Pastel shades lead
slowly conquering the sight
towards the masterpiece
soft intensity, soft saturation.

Time

Although hundreds of generations
wanted to control human fate,
there is an only revelation
and this is no straight.

We only belong to Nature
who are we apart from,
from ages to centuries,
more and more dumb.

Rushing and hurrying,
just worried about time,
our cruel owner
planning its next crime.

Innocence and penitence

Something dies inside me
making me harder,
stronger.
Hidden innocence
deeping and wonder.
Just overcoming
the punch of the life.

Now, I already have nothing,
but myself.
Now, I already have nothing,
but my dreams.